G16512

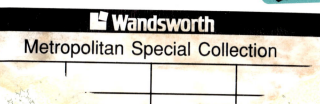

To the War with Waugh

The Author

JOHN ST JOHN

To the War
with Waugh

With an Introductory Memoir by
Christopher Hollis
and illustrations by Peter MacKarell

THE WHITTINGTON PRESS

Printed and published in Great Britain
by The Whittington Press,
BCM-Whittington, London WCIV 6XX

The opening pages and a few other parts of this
book originally appeared as a feature article in the
Sunday Times. They are reproduced by kind permission of Mr Harold Evans, its editor.

The quotations from Evelyn Waugh's novels are
reproduced by kind permission of A. D. Peters
and Company and the page references refer to the
Penguin editions.

Also by John St John:

Roast Beef and Pickles
A Trick of the Sun
Surgeon at Arms (with Daniel Paul)
Probation - The Second Chance
Alphabets and Reading (with Sir James Pitman)

Introductory Memoir

W H E N the war broke out Waugh rang me on the telephone and suggested that I should apply to join the same unit as he. I rejected the invitation on the pretext that I was already a member of the Officers' Emergency Reserve and therefore under obligation to wait for orders and then go wherever authority might see fit to send me. I was very well aware that this was untrue and that authority would be only too pleased if I could make any arrangements of service for myself. My real reason was that I feared that a war fought with Evelyn as a companion would be a war beyond my means. In this fear I was certainly right.

I therefore have the disadvantage in respect of Mr St John that I did not share with Evelyn the experience of the war, yet I have the advantage of having known Evelyn throughout a very much longer period - in fact ever since our undergraduate days. I would say of him that he had no liking for tranquillity. He liked life to be full of disturbance. The general fashion of undergraduate and Oxford Union opinion immediately after the war was that of liberal apology for the war and the Treaty of Versailles. We debated with a certain sanctimonious self-righteousness, 'That in the opinion of this House the French and the Russian governments were as guilty of the war as the German' - everybody, it seems, except ourselves. Evelyn came down to the debate and in rollicking spirit delivered a violent speech in favour of hate. It was our hate alone, he said, which gave us the spirit of adventure during the war. What exactly he meant by hating the Germans was indeed not very easy to see. He had no particular knowledge of what the Germans did during the war. He in no way objected to the Germans for being good Germans. They were as entitled to hate us as we were to hate them. Such antagonism made for more abundant, vigorous and meaningful life all round. It is typical of this spirit of chaotic disorder that his *Vile Bodies* ends in the news that a new European War has broken out but does not explain who that war is between, still less what is the cause of it.

Immediately after finishing his Oxford career Evelyn was in a very depressed mood as he reveals in his description in *A Little Learning*: his own suicide was only prevented by the intervention of a jellyfish. At that time, as a very dim preparatory schoolmaster he did not see any great prospect of winning success or even a respectable livelihood and in the first of his novels, *Decline and Fall*, the amusement of life mainly depends on the injustice and zany violence that is rife in it. It would be absurd to deduce from this book any high Tory aristocratic principles. The upper classes are indeed there - in the members of the Bollinger Club at Scone College at Oxford - but their conduct even by Waughean standards is in no way admirable. He celebrates the sound 'of the English upper classes baying for broken glass' as he contemplates their excesses, and the character who suffers injustice is the middle class character - Paul Pennyfeather. At that time we might say of him that he liked and betrayed his liking for a life of violence but that there was no question of any justice or principles in it. The life of the characters in these early novels was essentially a nihilistic life. He, like the rest of us, was of course quite without religion, and, although from his anglo-catholic upbringing by a pious father it was more natural for him than it would have been for most of his contemporaries to bring in religious references - the fact, for instance, that in *Decline and Fall* it is mentioned that Philbrick was a Roman Catholic, or the introduction of Father Rothschild or Mrs Ape and her 'angels' into *Vile Bodies* - it is never suggested that the claims of religion are taken at all seriously.

In 1931 he was received by Father Martin D'Arcy into the Catholic Church, but this conversion made no great immediate difference to his writing nor in any way abated his liking for the depiction of life as a charade of nihilistic violence. I remember the vigour with which he once quarrelled with me when I said that I hoped that the country might solve its industrial problems without a recourse to open violence. Indeed Ernest Oldmeadow, at that time editor of the Catholic *Tablet*, took his good faith very seriously to task in denunciation of the unedifying nature of his writings in *Black Mischief*. He was not at that or any other time a party politician. If he might be called a conservative he was only a conservative in so far as he had a contempt for the fashionable liberal slogans of the day or for any belief that they were at all likely to bring the peace and the tranquillity which they promised. Though later in life he travelled very widely, at the time of his undergraduate days he had never been abroad at all and was sometimes at little pains to conceal his resentment of his friends whose good fortune had enabled them at least to cross the Channel. When he began to travel he liked for choice to go to little known places well off the tourist map such as British Guiana, as it then was. He developed a pretence that he could not bear meals unless they were served to him by a negro waiter. In an article which he at that time wrote for the *Daily Mail* he committed himself to the very calculated extravagance that it was a great tragedy that slavery for negroes had ever been abolished. It was in this, as in much else, often difficult to know of his opinions whether they were sincere or designedly invented *pour épater le bourgeois*. At this stage of his life he thought the bitch goddess, success, important and, in order to obtain success, publicity was necessary. He was prepared to say and to do many extravagant things in order to obtain that success which in later life he was to come so heartily to despise.

The first evidence that he ever gave, I fancy, of any serious opinions on any question of foreign politics was over the Italian invasion of Abyssinia. In his passion to visit any strange and out of the way place he had already visited Abyssinia at the time of the Emperor Haile Selassie's coronation. Readers will remember the picture of that country, disguised as Azania, in *Black Mischief*. The Abyssinian war gave him another opportunity. As one of the few English writers who had any previous acquaintance with the country he was well qualified to report the war as a correspondent and he did so for the *Daily Mail*. Students will remember his interpretation of that war in *Waugh in Abyssinia*. His dislike of the liberal flattery of Haile Selassie, his contempt for non-European attempts at aping Europeans' ways, his contention, true or false, that Haile Selassie, thinly disguised as Seth in *Scoop*, used the patter of liberalism but in fact reformed nothing, caused him vigorously to support the Italian cause and to see in the Italians with their willingness to work with their hands on the land a superiority as colonists over the English and the French, interested only in exploitation through organisation. He was by no means a Fascist in Italy where he had at that time lived for a period in his mother-in-law's house at Rapallo and was repelled by the absurdity of the Fascist leaders' barbarous and bombastic oratory. He had no liking for Sir Oswald Mosley but he disliked liberalism even more.

A somewhat similar sort of errand at about the same time took him to Mexico, where he wrote a book, *Robbery Under Law*, in exposure of the alleged hypocrisy of the Socialist leaders there. There is some mystery about this book. It was alleged that he wrote it at the subvention of the American oil interests. He never confessed as much but he was certainly not very proud of the whole transaction and always afterwards omitted *Robbery Under Law* from his list of published works. Certainly his was not the sort of conservatism that would have any natural sympathy with international financial corporations.

When the Spanish war broke out he, unlike most English writers, gave his support to the cause of General Franco. It was not, I fancy, that he had any special illusions about those who were fighting for Franco, Spanish officers or aristocrats, but those opposed to Franco were to his judgement still less attractive. When he was received into the Catholic Church by Father D'Arcy his catholicism was, as he once confessed to me, sincere but not all-embracing. He was not *engagé*. It did not, for instance, betray itself in his writing. Father D'Arcy was at that time the Rector of Campion Hall at Oxford and as an act of gratitude Evelyn wrote the life of Edmund Campion, the Elizabethan Jesuit, and gave to Campion Hall all the proceeds from the work. It was his study of Campion, his discovery of a man who thought that all must be sacrificed for religion, which was the great turning point in his life. Thenceforward, whatever his practice, the cause of religion was the one cause which he admitted as worthy of sacrifice and on that test, whatever the failings of Franco and his followers, there could be no doubt that Franco's enemies, the so-called Loyalists, were the enemies of religion, the murderers of priests and nuns. They were to be opposed. Yet even then the position was not easy. It was not perhaps easy to see in General Franco the pure Christian crusader. It was less easy to find such characteristics in Mussolini. It was quite impossible to find them in Hitler and in the years before the war the judgements on international politics were not easy for him any more than they were for that very different person, George Orwell, from whom he differed on almost every other topic but was at one with him on this alone. Mussolini was a man of mixed good and bad and there were some decent elements in the Fascist régime, but it was not important. Hitler was important and wholly evil. But then so was Stalin. His dilemma was the dilemma which he ascribes to Guy Crouchback in *Men at Arms*. We were indeed going to fight against evil but in asking for a Russian alliance we were only too ready to fight against evil in the company of evil. To Evelyn, as to Crouchback, the news of the Soviet-Nazi pact, the news that all the evil would be against us was an undiluted relief.

I think that Mr St John does not quite sufficiently draw the distinction between his earlier mood of enthusiasm and the later cynicism about the British cause. It was in the earlier mood that he wrote *Put Out More Flags*, dedicating it to Randolph Churchill and hailing 'the Churchillian renaissance that was abroad'. The war effort at that time was only to be criticised in so far as it was insufficient. It was in his later spirit that he wrote of Guy Crouchback's disgust at the cynical sacrifice of the Jews in Yugoslavia who had been evicted from their homes, of the war in which the price of victory would be a world made safe for Trimmer and for Hooper, 'the inevitable betrayal of civilised values', as Mr St John puts it.

Evelyn, Mr St John describes as a man cynical about the details of regimental etiquette. This was, I think, true of the Waugh of the later years of the war rather than of the earlier. In those earlier years he rather prided himself on his military bearing and spoke with respect of such things as the obligation of official secrecy. Later, both in life and in his writings he viewed the debased society of men who, like Rex Mottram in *Brideshead Revisited* were 'not all there', with a jaundiced eye. His writings and his own company were mainly among the titled to an extent that was curious in a man of such wide interests and himself of no aristocratic birth. But he had no illusions about the virtues of the aristocracy. The Flytes of Brideshead are not an edifying family. He was faithful to the Church but with the reforms of the Vatican council he thought it had in a manner abandoned him. Guy Crouchback's old Catholic father was his ideal character and he recounts in a moving fashion his pious and religious funeral but then adds in the later edition the sad footnote, 'Most of these ceremonies have by now been abolished'.

Christopher Hollis

To the War with Waugh

DUNKIRK, TOBRUK, D-DAY, ARNHEM...the wide screen, trendy TV editing, yet another 'authentic memoir' add an attractive and misleading gloss to the reality. After thirty years the moods of 1939-45 are so glamourised and distorted by the needs of sedentary entertainment that they are unrecognisable. A nostalgia is created for drama that never was. The early months, that grey, frozen winter of the phoney war – or the 'Great Bore War' as they called it – was in particular lacking in glory or goggle-box appeal. The black-out and ration books were novel but not exciting. My generation was not anxious to be heroes. We didn't go blithely to war as did our fathers in 1914, nor did we suffer their illusions. Throughout the 1930s we'd hoped and tried to kid ourselves it wouldn't happen; and when it did we joined up – or for the most part were called up – unwillingly but with resignation.

This at any rate was how I felt myself and I doubt if I differed much from most others in their early twenties. At the time of Abyssinia and of Munich you could say I was something of a premature anti-Fascist, but when the lights finally went out I certainly lacked eagerness to be a hero or even to put on uniform. The manner of my eventual enlistment was unusual – some might call it peculiar, even hilarious – yet I have always felt it was typical of the war's first twilit, panicky, intensly amateurish phase. Rather than wait to be called up I decided to volunteer, but this was merely because it seemed the best way of avoiding being shoved into the infantry or something equally tedious and dangerous. Systematically I assessed the appeals for service volunteers in the press or on the BBC and submitted an application for anything that sounded moderately interesting and, above all, safe. Physically and spiritually, I knew I was not cut out for the cockpit of a Spitfire, or the belly of a submarine, or the turret of a tank. Some of us had to serve our country in the pay corps, the ack-ack, intelligence, signals, catering ... and why not therefore me? I wasn't less patriotic than most of us. Let's put it down to enlightened self-interest.

Among the softer options I applied for was one described in the advertisement as a 'marine naval base'. This had a comfortable and

I

tolerably safe ring and I have always enjoyed shipping and ports. So far none of my offers to help my country had been taken up and so it was with surprise and satisfaction that I received a summons by return of post to attend two days later for an interview at the Admiralty itself. My hair freshly cut and wearing my latest fifty-shilling-tailor suit, I reported at the main entrance in Whitehall and was shown into an elegant room occupied by an officer talking on the telephone. As he waved me into an armchair I spotted enough red tabs and crossed swords to suggest that he was pretty important. He was in fact a major-general and adjutant-general of the entire corps of Royal Marines.

Waiting nervously for the call to end I sensed there had been a mistake, that I'd been ushered into the wrong office while the expected visitor, probably at least an under-secretary of state, was being interviewed by a recruiting sergeant in the basement. But not at all. The telephone call finished, the general rapidly found

2

my name on the list on his blotter and grinned a welcome, but then the telephone rang again. It must have rung at least five more times during the course of my interview and during the brief periods between calls there was time only to confirm the details of my education, to agree that I'd served in my school's officers' training corps and passed Certificate A (Part I only), and to be asked what games I most enjoyed. Fortunately my mumbling about a 'spot of mountain walking and an occasional swim' was lost in the clangour of the next telephone call.

This time it was an immediate summons to visit what can only have been the First Lord himself if not the War Cabinet, and with an apologetic handshake the general hurried to the door: 'Sorry to dash but my colonel will put you in the picture. In the next room - through there. Tell him I sent you.'

This room was a little smaller but the colonel was equally red-tabbed and impressive. His voice was traditionally clipped and fruity. 'You're a lucky fellow! Let me be the first to congratulate you. It's not everyone who's chosen for this particular outfit and no wonder! It's the most exciting and hazardous in the entire arm-ed forces.' Surely, I ventured, there must really be a mistake, but the colonel wouldn't hear of it. 'Anyone he sends in here is auto-matically taken on strength, subject of course to a medical but you look fit enough. He tells the rejects they'll hear later and person-ally I never clap eyes on them.'

I mentioned the marine naval base. Could this really be so hazardous? At this the colonel was obviously perplexed. 'Never heard of it. Must be some other show. The task allotted to your outfit will be to raid the enemy's coastline - go in under cover of darkness. Establish a temporary beach-head . . . that sort of thing. We're building some special armoured craft that will put you ashore whether it's beaches, seaweed-covered rocks, or cliffs. Come back for you 24 hours, maybe 48 hours later . . . those of you, that is, who can still make it . . .'

That was October 1939 and the term 'commando' had not yet been adopted. Security had scarcely been thought of and, walking

3

in unchecked from the street, I might have been a Nazi spy - in fact I wasn't, having at that time an affection for the revolutionary Left.

'Once ashore you will make your way inland to blow up a Hun power station, wreck a railway viaduct, pinch a few Hun prisoners, or what have you. One of the first jobs we're thinking of is a surprise landing at this end of the Kiel Canal. Our long-haired chappies have cooked up a new sort of underwater mine. Guaranteed to smash the stoutest lock gates.' My further, by now frantic attempts to raise doubts and questions were brushed aside. 'The Old Man' - he meant Winston Churchill, then in charge of the Admiralty - 'is taking a special interest in this new outfit. Wants regular reports.' Standing up, the colonel grabbed my hand. 'Once again my congratulations. You'll be gazetted ten days from now. Rank of Second Lieutenant. No time to bother with OCTUs. We need you quick.'

I was in. Ten days later I set off at dawn for Victoria Station. I was dressed in officers' khaki service drill, I grasped a leather-covered cane, and clumped along in painful army boots - the list of equipment that came with my £40 draft and the names of recognised outfitters omitted to mention that off the parade-ground officers wore 'Shoes, walking, brown'. As I followed the porter wheeling my luggage, I was alarmed to find ordinary soldiers, naval ratings, even some WRENs, saluting me. Feeling an imposter I returned the compliment gravely, but with the wrong (Naval) kind of salute.

At divisional headquarters in Chatham the welcome could not have been friendlier. In the officers' mess a pink gin was placed in my hand by a jolly captain who introduced me to several other second lieutenants who were joining the same day. Altogether there were fourteen of us. The general's taste must have been eclectic for we were a peculiar assortment physiques, professions, and ages. Among them was a solicitor, a sports journalist, a banker, an enormous flushed gentleman who was a wine merchant, and a prep. school master with an Earl Haig moustache. I was the youngest

4

and the eldest was thirty-six: a short, peppery-looking person called Evelyn Waugh - another reason for now thinking my experience may have been peculiar, yet in the truest sense they were 'universal' because without knowing it I had also become a Halberdier.

Unused to gin, I soon felt very much at ease as I was introduced to various officers who were crowding into the mess for their pre-lunch noggins. It was only when listening to a middle-aged major describe the characteristics of the local golf course that I began to realise that in a subtle way I was dressed differently from all the other officers. Where they had three buttons I had four; the V-shaped braid piping on my cuffs pointed the wrong way; there was something funny about my lapels. My tailor had followed an out-of-date pattern. An unfortunate start but everyone was very decent

5

about it. It was considered a splendid joke except by my batman. Old enough to be my father and accustomed to tending peacetime regulars in a crack regiment, it must have distressed him to be landed with such an obviously temporary, acting officer and gentleman. His first glance must have told him that I would never achieve the smartness and swagger that was *de rigueur* whether off duty or on the parade-ground.

It was here that we spent most of our time, in a squad of fourteen marching back and forth under the orders of a colour-sergeant (Colour-Sergeant Cork in Waugh's *Men at Arms*). We might be second lieutenants and elsewhere he would stiffen at our approach and salute us with drill-book perfection, but under his control on the parade-ground we were treated for once as what we really were: the rawest of recruits. 'Lieutenant Wuff, press on that rifle butt and keep your precious eyes to the front. To the *front* I said! You're not 'ere to collect daisies!'

As the Panzer divisions marshalled themselves in the forests beyond the Maginot Line and the Finns slowly fell back before the Russians, we marched and turned, we marched and wheeled, sloped and presented antique rifles, had the length of our pace measured with the colour-sergeant's long wooden drill-ground callipers. The nearest we ever got to warfare was 'aircraft drill'. We would be marching in column of threes along a road on the outskirts of Chatham when, without warning, our instructor would yell: 'H'aircraft approaching from the right!' We would then come to a smart halt and, standing upright on the crown of the road, raise our rifles by numbers and send up an imaginary 'cone of fire'. The method was similar to that employed to shoot pheasants with shot guns. Aimed ahead of the propeller, the pilot would fly into our cone of fourteen bullets, one of which with reasonable luck would penetrate his temple and the plane would descend, a screaming ball of flames and smoke.

We were certainly kept busy what with elementary tactics; with corps history, learned by rote with snap questions about the date of the capture of Gibraltar and our privilege to march through the

6

City of London with fixed bayonets; there was a daily session in the gym which Evelyn in particular hated - when unwatched, he delighted in what he called his 'energy-saving Bedaux system' of arm-stretching and trunk-bending; and of course we were expected to take advantage of the amenities open to members of the mess - enormous sirloins, home-made game pies, a new Stilton each Monday, silver candelabra mirrored in the mahogany, marvellous vintage port; guest nights every fortnight with an excruciating Royal Marine string orchestra playing *The Chocolate Soldier*; golf, billiards, bridge, but - because of the war - no polo. In most other ways the war just had not reached this military hide-out.

OF COURSE THIS KIND OF LIFE WAS NOT TO LAST
and we were soon moved to a deserted holiday camp at Kingswood,
near Deal. The winter was severe and we slept in unheated chalets,
assembling in an empty Victorian mansion for meals, lectures, and
of course gin - in his novel Waugh called it Kut-al-Imara House,
though I don't remember the incident of the 'thunder-box'. We'd
been joined by newly enlisted temporary officers from the other
Royal Marine divisions as well as some of the regular captains,
majors, and colonels who were to form the skeleton of the R M
brigade. In command was a brigadier with a boyish but manic
laugh who, it was believed, had been selected for his reputation for
dare-devil escapades - clearly the prototype for Evelyn's Ritchie-
Hook. In lectures he promised us plenty of blood and confirmed
that our prime role would be to mount seaborne raids on the
enemy's coastline.

Most of our time however was now taken up with sand-table exercises and TEWTs - tactical exercises without troops - based on the lessons learned in 1914-18, on India's North-West frontier, at Omdurman or fighting the Matabele. In small shivering groups, clutching our virgin map-cases and chinagraph pencils, we took turns at describing how we would capture a farmhouse or copse on the next Kentish ridge: the route of the assault party, the lines of enfilading fire, the positioning of smoke bombs. As with Ritchie-Hook, tactics were interpreted as the 'art of biffing. Defence was studied cursorily and only as the period of reorganization between two bloody assaults. . . . Long raw misty days were passed in the surrounding country with maps and binoculars. Sometimes they stood on the beach and biffed imaginary defenders into the hills; sometimes they biffed imaginary invaders from the hills into the sea. They invested downland hamlets and savagely biffed imaginary hostile inhabitants. Sometimes they merely collided with imaginary rivals for the use of the main road and biffed them out of

the way.'* We practised receiving orders from a company commander, synchronising watches, going forward to make our own reconnaissances, 'appreciating the situation' from both our own and the enemy's points of view, and finally giving orders ourselves to imaginary platoon sergeants and section corporals. We were taught that, to be successful, tactics depended on a rigorous routine of analysis, an invariable sequence of self-questioning: 'What is my intention?' 'Is there more than one way of achieving it?' 'What courses are open to the enemy?' and so on. Applied intelligently, the procedure was undoubtedly effective and after thirty years I still find it helps to apply the same military logic to everyday personal dilemmas.

Sharing instruction and lectures and the icy discomforts of those

*Men at Arms, p. 140

holiday camp chalets with sixty fellow second lieutenants came close to my periodic nightmares of being back at boarding school and, like Guy Crouchback, I was often secretly miserable. Quite a few, including some in their late twenties, appeared to enjoy reverting to the swashbuckling, debagging boisterousness of the upper-school changing-room - qualities apt, no doubt, for our role as a ruthless raiding force and for what our instructors called 'grabbing the Hun by his bollocks'. Most evenings were spent bellowing rugger club songs, favourites being *They're Shifting Father's Grave to Build a Sewer*, the *Sexual Alphabet* that ends with '... Z for the Zambuk he rubs on his tool', and the *One-Armed Flautist*, that 'innocently obscene performance' staged by Major Tickeridge of the Halberdiers.

Respite came with an occasional quiet evening out with the portly wine merchant and Evelyn Waugh who'd got themselves elected honorary members of the Deal Constitutional club. In an

elder brotherly way Evelyn seemed to like me because he also took me to a small Italian restaurant still open on the front; I enjoyed the cooking quite as much as Guy Crouchback, though I don't think it was really called The Garibaldi. Over our *risotto con funghi* I remember him telling me that my companionship was a relief after most of our colleagues. Though of course flattered, this was difficult to credit, especially as we seemed to disagree on so many fundamentals. But antagonism itself can provide a bond. His extreme reactionary posture was the mirror-image of my own youthful leftism which he was quick enough to notice though, because of cowardice and self-doubt, I kept this muted - not that politics were often discussed in the mess. Impatiently, but not maliciously, he was scornful of my affection for *The New Statesman* and recommended *The Tablet* as a substitute; he scoffed at the perseverance with which I was then reading a somewhat progressive, dryasdust *Outline of Modern Knowledge* published by Gollancz. He was of course a passionate supporter of the Finns as they astonishingly resisted the Russians at the Mannerheim Line. He longed to be there, though he confessed his worst nightmare was to be left

lying wounded in the Finnish snow and eventually picked up by a Soviet medical team and bandaged by a *female* Red Army doctor. Death would be preferable. Death, I recall, also came into our conversation when, after describing the difficulties of getting his first marriage annulled in Rome and the ridiculous fees charged by the Vatican lawyers, he assured me that before I was much older I would forsake my lukewarm, ill-defined Protestant Agnosticism for Rome.

'Just wait until you meet a real personal crisis or look your own death in the face for the first time. When that happens we haven't a choice.'

IN THE SPRING WE WENT UNDER CANVAS AT BISLEY, near Aldershot, and there we met our NCOs, for the most part regulars, and the other-rank Marines who like ourselves were HOs - 'Hostilities Only'. At just twenty-three I found myself in charge of the lives of thirty men armed with rifles, three Bren machine-guns, a cumbersome anti-tank rifle, and a two-inch mortar like a drainpipe that lobbed small explosive bombs and canisters of smoke. My only personal weapon was a Smith and Wesson revolver with which to my chagrin I couldn't count on hitting a beer bottle at a range of eight feet. Compared with my five months' service, my men could boast a mere six weeks but they already looked and behaved (at least on the camp parade-ground) not unlike seasoned troops - thanks to Sergeant Smith (his real name) whose experience, skill and tact were to guide me in so many predicaments. As *Men at Arms* makes clear, the normal relationship between 'platoon commander and sergeant was that of child and nannie. The sergeant should keep his officer out of mischief. The officer's job was to sign things, to take the blame and quite simply to walk ahead and get shot first. And, as an officer, he should have a certain intangibility belonging, as in old-fashioned households, to the further side of the baize-doors.'*

Saluting, Sergeant Smith would set an example of instant, unquestioning, proud obedience and faith in my sagacity; yet when I was about to commit a blunder he knew just how to whisper a fatherly warning without anyone else noticing. If he ever felt resentment at my inexperience, my lack of military talent or even inclinations being given precedence over his own twelve years of loyal service as a regular, well all I can say is that he never showed it. He accepted without question the void between the officers' and sergeants' messes, the authority symbolised by the single pip on my epaulet and by my leather-covered swagger-cane; indeed it was he who showed me, tactfully as always, the division between our roles, that it was my job ultimately to utter com-

Men at Arms, p. 172

mands (albeit with his prompting) and his to see that they were bloody well carried out, that he was a buffer between me and the other ranks, and that if it was a case of extra punitive parades, or cajoling at the end of a thirty-mile route march, or of organizing the digging of latrines when the rest of the company had shore (i.e. Woking) leave, the responsibility was his, not mine. An officer, he believed, should get to know his men as individuals and take a paternal and helpful interest in their personal problems, yet at the same time he should remain aloof. When, for example, our platoon was once detailed to unload a trainful of ammunition and I began to lend a hand with lifting the boxes onto trucks, he took me aside and warned that by doing so I was demeaning myself and was in danger of losing the men's respect.

Inevitably Sergeant Smith and I had our differences, the most serious being over drill - not that he shared anything with the bellowing clown-bully of tradition, though we had some of these

17

as well. The company commanders and most of my brother platoon officers also attached extraordinary, fetishist importance to
the precise angle of a shouldered rifle butt and to the accuracy with
which their marching columns wheeled, left-inclined, and turned
in the manner of infantry in the time of Marlborough. I confess to
having at first relished barking-out orders, but it was the petty
power of a uniformed prefect and unlikely to foster the self-
reliance and initiative which would clearly be needed when fanning
out in the dark, under fire to establish a beach-head perimeter. Indeed it was noticeable that the longer they drilled, the more sullen
and unco-operative my men became, whereas they eagerly took

part in sessions devoted to handling weapons, distance judging, digging positions with entrenching tools, camouflage, stalking under cover - these came closer to the real thing, to why they'd readily, though reluctantly, left homes and girl-friends. Whenever possible therefore I cut down on the four or more hours of obligatory drilling until, eventually, after a hot afternoon of observing and tracking games in the Bisley Common heather, I told the platoon that if in future they were always prepared to drill as if it were the King's Birthday, we would reduce the time spent on the parade-ground to an hour a day.

'As you say, sir!' Sergeant Smith looked bewildered and his salute was subtly reproachful but he co-operated loyally and so did the men. During that one hour they were soon drilling to perfection and before we left Bisley we came top in the battalion drill contest.

Very much against his wishes, Evelyn had been roped in as the battalion correspondent to *The Globe and Laurel*, the Royal Marines' house journal. In the April 1940 issue, among pages of pedestrian accounts of football matches and sergeants' mess socials, there is a short anonymous, but inimitable report of our arrival '. . . in a landscape of burned gorse and immature conifers, prettily embellished with spent cartridge cases . . . after dark some battalions are said to devote themselves primarily to the larger aspects of war, debating the effects of Roumanian policy upon the Anatolian jute industry, while others, more, or perhaps, less practical, wander through the marshes in darkness or threaten late visitors to the mess with fixed bayonets . . . Moustaches are growing luxuriantly, coughs are on the decline; battle dress lends a menacing aspect to the most peaceable characters.'

Evelyn himself had a new moustache, bristly and clipped short, which enhanced his customary choleric mien. My own despite stiffening with Hungarian pomade, was resolutely unmilitary. Although the R M Brigade's role was identical to that of the commandos, who were to become notorious for their lack of conventional military bullshit, we were still a crack regiment to whose customs I was ludicrously unsuited. I managed well enough when it came to manoeuvres, mock-fighting and maintaining discipline, but the achievement of a smart, martial appearance was still quite beyond me; despite the services of a batman (now a young HO who in the field was also my personal runner), I was frequently in trouble with the adjutant because of the angle of my blue fore-and-aft cap (or 'cunt cap') or for showing too big a loop on my shoulder lanyard. Throughout my war service such problems plagued me so that much later on the colonel, despite recommending my promotion to captain, felt bound to write in my confidential report (which I saw and initialled) that I was 'the most slovenly dressed officer ever to serve under my command'.

Worse, I was blind to shortcomings in the uniform and equipment of the other ranks. At inspections I would walk slowly along the rigid lines, hoping franticly to detect an undone button, a strap or pouch whose webbing was imperfectly blancoed, a boot with an

unpolished sole (sic). Once as battalion orderly officer I had to deputise for the adjutant at the morning ceremony of changing the HQ guard. Though hours would be spent in perfecting their turnout, I knew that the adjutant would invariably discover sufficient minor sartorial lapses to justify the award of extra parades to at least four out of a guard of nine. Accompanied by the regimental sergeant-major, I therefore subjected each guard to the most searching scrutiny but as usual could find nothing amiss.

'Pardon me, sir, for reminding you,' the R S M muttered as we faced each other motionlessly at attention, 'but no extra parades? Means, sir, creating a precedent. Never happened, sir, not with the HQ guard, not in my twenty-four years service it hasn't!'

To my shame I stalked back along the line and singled out for punishment three men at random.

We were still at Bisley when the German offensive pronged through Belgium and the evacuation began from Dunkirk. Despite the propaganda ballyhoo most of us at the time, especially the more senior regular officers, recognised it to be the rout it really was. Although our serious training as a formation had scarcely begun, the débâcle meant that we were now potential first line troops and indeed during one night the second R M battalion disappeared from the next-door camp site to occupy an undefended Iceland. The fighting in France nevertheless still seemed remote and our main anxieties centred on the size of the next cigarette issue and the chances of week-end leave. The pristine enthusiasm of the HOs was already a little tarnished, though the addition of a couple of long-service, sea-going Marines to each platoon was intended to strengthen our lilywhite ranks with experience and reliability. In practice their influence undermined the battalion's eagerness even further because detachment commanders throughout the Home Fleet had seen it as a chance to dispose of their most troublesome 'lower-deck lawyers' and scrimshankers.

Whether regular or HO, scarcely anyone in my platoon seemed to have much idea of the reasons for the war's outbreak or why they were fighting it. Anti-fascism was still almost a dirty word.

The invasion of Abyssinia, the Spanish Civil War, the falling bastions in Austria and Czechoslovakia, the Nazi persecution of Jews and democrats had largely passed them by. Hitler was merely an up-to-date Kaiser Bill with a funny moustache and the 'only good Hun was a dead one'. I began to understand how it was - if not why - our fathers' generation had been so ready to die in their hundred thousands in the Flanders mud, albeit gallantly but without being given proper reasons. To make my men more aware and therefore, I believed, better fighters, I gave occasional lecturettes

to explain how Europe was now menaced by an unprecedented type of barbarity, but their eyes would soon glaze with boredom and I'm sure I sounded a pompous prig.

Despite the endless saluting and senseless square-bashing, quite a few of the officers, including my own (regular) company commander, acquired a talent for winning the HOs' confidence and genuine respect. Not so Evelyn who, once away from the officers' mess marquee, seemed to delight in aping Lord Cardigan. Because of Evelyn's greater age (and maybe his connections) he was the only temporary officer at that early period to be made a captain and given command of a company, but he handled its members with contempt relieved only by avuncular patronage. A petty offence could make him apoplectic. I once heard him address a parade on the question of swearing: 'The continued use of obscenities in conversation is tedious and undignified. These words punctuate your speech like a hiccup. Instead they should be savoured and reserved for the creative act itself or for moments of the most extreme frustration.' As they listened dutifully to the petulant, elegant voice the ranks of motionless faces were bewildered and uncomprehending. Evelyn certainly lived up to his reputation for snobbery, though it struck me as being in part ironical, if not a pose. In the mess as well as on the parade ground he treated inferiors in rank - or superiors without the right social background - with a scorn that while amusing was uncharitable; but this also made him impervious to too much military bullshit. Personally I couldn't help revelling in his companionship and found him a delightful fellow sufferer, especially when we were messed about unnecessarily or when conditions were physically unpleasant.

Bisley provided the background for parts of *Put out More Flags*. It was on nearby Chobham Common that poor Mr Smallwood's platoon put down smoke and there was the map-reading muddle over the third E and the B in 'Bee Garden'.* Much of our time was taken up with route marches and increasingly elaborate battalion and brigade exercises. Our steel helmets ornamented with bracken, we enacted the assaults which awaited us. Umpires would appear from behind gorse bushes, throw a couple of thunder flashes and inform tired, incomprehending Marines that they were

Put Out More Flags, p. 130

24

either dead or wounded. The day invariably ended with what the CO called 'another bloody awful shambles', what with units arriving at the wrong rendezvous or firing blank cartridges at their own side. It was after such a débâcle and we'd returned exhausted and filthy to camp to enjoy cool beer and buckets of hot water provided by our batmen that the CO tore a strip off us for seeing to our own comfort before our men's. He was furious. Standing at attention in a semi-circle in front of his bell-tent office, it was impressed upon us that inspection of the men's rifles, checking their feet for blisters, and supervision of their evening meal was an essential prior duty for anyone privileged to call himself a Royal Marine officer.

'Any questions?'

It was a solemn moment and the enquiry was itself clearly rhetorical, but Evelyn was undaunted: 'Would you not agree, sir, that it would be ever so much nicer if there were no Marine soldiers and if everyone could be an officer?'

Our CO was a very tolerant man with a sense of humour but this kind of provocation was difficult to take. Evelyn could seldom resist the temptation to poke fun: for example, I once heard him innocently enquire, to the perplexity of a pompous visiting brass-hat, if it were true that 'in the Roumanian army no one beneath the rank of major is permitted to use lipstick'.

Several hours a week were spent learning to handle our weapons on the Bisley rifle ranges. Squatting by each man in turn, I managed to provide passably convincing instruction in how to lie properly on the stomach, grip the barrel, align the sights and 'squeeze' the trigger. Most of the platoon improved rapidly and the butts were soon signalling back plenty of magpies and bulls. At the end of one morning's practice the company sergeant-major suggested that the platoon officers might like to fire a few rounds themselves. Watched by a hundred men standing at ease behind the firing-point, the three officer-experts took painstaking aim: my colleagues performed creditably enough, but my best shot was an outer and with four out of ten shots the waving flag from the butts signalled that I'd missed the target completely.

On night exercises, stumbling among the pines and heather with the aid of luminous compasses, the map-reading blunders and mistimings provided the most telling reminder of our military rawness. Darkness also undermined discipline. During one all-night scheme on a golf course the arrival of the midnight rum issue at the portly wine merchant's platoon HQ by the eleventh tee led to the hilarious abandonment of weapons and positions, just as the opposing 'Redland' launched a surprise attack. It was while dug in for the night on an imaginary beachhead a few miles to the NW of Woking that I too was faced with my first serious breach of military regulations.

Rain thickened the blackness. Apart from outlying sentries, the men lay in the bracken bivouacked in pairs beneath tents made from two groundsheets. As the officer I enjoyed a single bivouac

erected by my batman a few yards away from the centre of the three sections. About two in the morning I was awakened by Sergeant Smith. Sticking my head out from beneath the groundsheet I could just make him out saluting at attention in the downpour. He was accompanied by two other rigid figures.

'Marine —, sir. Put in a request, sir, to see you urgently. A complaint, sir. Personal business, but he's fully entitled under Admiralty regulations. Matter's sort of delicate, sir, you might say.' When I asked if it couldn't wait till we'd got back to camp or at any rate until it grew light or stopped raining, the reply was monitory as well as respectful. 'Delay might be unwise, sir. Could turn out very tricky.'

Marine — was then ordered to take six paces nearer my head, to salute, repeat his name and regimental number. A pale gangling Londoner with an outsize nose, he was clearly very distressed: 'It's Corporal —, sir. Asked me to share his bivouac, sir, sort of special like. Kipped down head to feet like what the sergeant said . . . I'd gone clean off, sir, before it started. . . . First, I thought it was one of those dirty dreams, sir.'

'Before *what* started?'

'The corporal, sir, like I said. Started fiddling with my flies and all that, sir.'

'Didn't you tell him to stop?'

'Course I did, sir. Told him it wasn't decent and he should know better an'all. Him a married man, what's more, with two lovely kiddies . . . but then when I kipped off again I woke up with his hand . . . if you'll pardon the expression, sir, his whole hand sort of worked its way inside, sir, taking a grab like . . . see what I mean, sir?'

Corporal — was next marched forward out of the darkness and after calling out his name and regimental number and being warned, very correctly, by Sergeant Smith that he was under no obligation to say anything, he bleakly admitted the charges. '. . . Don't know, sir, what came over me. . . . Never happened before, sir. . . . Sort of an impulse, you might say, sir, what with being shacked up so close together to keep warm. . . .'

28

Bewildered, I had no inkling of what I ought to do. Nothing like this had been so much as hinted at during our training lectures. At my public school there had been regular expulsions for homosexuality but it had all passed me by. I suppose I couldn't have been very attractive to the homos, nor can I recall passing through the traditional pre-pubescent homo phase myself, though on a pre-war holiday in Paris I'd been befriended by an entertaining roué called Brian Howard who'd taken me to a queers' night-club and who'd taught me to be tolerant. But neither Sergeant Smith nor I had yet heard of Kinsey and it was seventeen years before Wolfenden.

'If I might suggest something, sir?' came the helpful mutter. 'You ought to put the accused under close arrest. At dawn we can have him marched back to camp under escort.'

It was my first arrest, though I'm glad to say that events led to the matter being hushed up. There was no time for the customary court-martial because forty-eight hours later the battalion was under immediate orders to move. The corporal merely lost his stripes and was returned to the R M depot at Deal for another posting. The battalion, its basic training incomplete, was needed for active service.

As the Germans assembled their great invasion fleet, each day brought news of Spitfires in battle above the Channel, of middle-aged and elderly volunteers parading with pikes, of S S troops being parachuted at night - usually disguised as nuns with machine-guns strapped beneath their habits. Everyone had their own leaked Fifth Column anecdote, each as extraordinary as the unbroken summer weather. The sun certainly shone with ironic holiday splendour as the 1st R M battalion entrained with all its stores and weapons for a stifling, jolting journey to a destination still on the secret list. In trains we were no exception to the troops in *Put out More Flags* who '. . . leave camp in a state of ceremonial smartness; they parade on the platform as though on the barrack square; they are detailed to their coaches and there a process of transformation and decay sets in; coats are removed, horrible packages of food appear, dense clouds of smoke obscure the windows, in a few minutes the floor is deep in cigarette ends, lumps of bread and meat, waste paper; in repose the bodies assume attitudes of extreme abandon. . . .'*

The anti-climax came when after passing Cardiff and Swansea we detrained at Haverfordwest where we were billeted in empty shops and warehouses. But after a week we marched to Pembroke Dock to board an ancient cross-channel steamer which had been used at Dunkirk, its decks and saloons still stained with blood. As slings of ammo boxes were lowered into the hold we had little doubt that it would soon be our turn, though, like Guy Crouch- back, we were astonished and depressed to learn that we would be heading for Eire. The plan was to forestall the Reichswehr which had eyes on her South and West coast anchorages as bases for U- boats and her East coast as a platform for the invasion of Britain's flank. Like the Halberdiers, we 'were at two hours' notice to sail. After two days orders were relaxed to allow troops in formed bodies ashore for training and recreation. They had to remain with- in sight of the mast of their ship, which would hoist a flag to summon them in case of immediate sailing orders.'†

The ship was disagreeably crowded and, literally, lousy, and at night many slept on deck. On the third afternoon we cast off and steamed down Milford Haven. At a conference in the second class saloon our company commander issued maps and explained our role in the investment of Cork - or was it Limerick? It proved of no significance because we were scarcely clear of St. Ann's Head before the ship turned round and headed back to Pembroke Dock where another train awaited to rush us to Cornwall. Our role as coastal invaders had been reversed. Within a few hours the entire R M brigade was deployed to defend a stretch of coast to the west of Plymouth. At twenty-three and with but seven months' military experience, with a force of thirty men, supplemented by a hundred

*Put Out More Flags, p. 214
†Men at Arms, p. 204

31

home guard, I was charged with denying to the enemy the headland and quays, the buildings and inhabitants of the holiday-fishing town of West Looe.

The Germans, we were told, might attempt to land at any moment and my orders were to take whatever emergency steps I decided necessary to ensure their repulsion. The locals, swelled by frightened middle-class, middle-aged and elderly refugees from London, were relieved to see us and made no demur as we hacked down trees to improve fields of fire, overturned lorries to make road-blocks, and, like Mr Smallwood's platoon, 'entered with relish into the work of destroying local amenities . . . lined the sands with barbed wire and demolished the steps leading from esplanade to beach . . . sandbagged the bow-windows of private houses'.* There'd been no time to arrange billets and because it offered a splendid position for a Bren gun to cover the harbour mouth, I decided to requisition half a fully occupied hotel for sleeping quarters and my own battle HQ. I was quite as astonished as the proprietor to hear myself giving the guests an hour's notice

*Put Out More Flags, p. 216

in which to evacuate their bedrooms - not that we got much sleep. Each night an hour before dawn, after a hard day of digging and camouflaging defences and tank traps, the whole platoon would be standing to by its weapons, peering out into the grey Channel mists for the first sign of the German armada.

Evelyn's (and Crouchback's) company were defending a neighbouring stretch of coast. Like them we had a surprise visit from an inspecting general who, I remember, congratulated us for camouflaging a section HQ as a refreshment hut:

' "Parachutes," said the general, "are the very devil. Well, remember. The positions are to be held to the last man and the last round."

' "Yes, sir," said Guy.

' "Do your men understand that?"

' "Yes, sir."

' "And remember, you must never speak of '*If* the enemy comes' but '*When* they come'. They are coming *here*, *this* month. Understand?" '*

Although my reason and the information and orders received from the company commander and the battalion HQ at inland Liskeard told me that their arrival was imminent, I never felt it as a possible reality. It was still an exciting, quite enjoyable grown-up game. The concept of live helmeted Germans pouring out of boats beneath my snugly sandbagged HQ and firing their way past the ice-cream kiosks and municipal public lavatory was just too ridiculous!

A week, two weeks, three, four, five . . . they'd still not come and the pre-dawn stand-to became an increasing drag. Though the men were still being stood pints in the town's pubs and were fast learning the soldierly expertise at coaxing housewives to provide fish suppers and their daughters to lower their knickers, our presence was now tolerated rather than welcomed. By what authority, people were asking, had all those trees come crashing down, all

*Men at Arms, p. 208

35

those front gardens been ravaged? When an unusually high tide
carried away the three rows of pointed stakes and Dannert wire
coils we'd so laboriously erected across the town's main beach, the
fishermen's quays were loud with lumbering Cornish wisecracks
and 'told-you-sos'. When a Verey cartridge was accidentally dis-
charged through a window of our hotel-billet to shower ruby
sparks over the guests taking tea on the patio, the proprietor's
complaints and demands for compensation released the concealed
outrage at our invasion of his premises. A few nights later there
was almost a much nastier accident. Sea-mist was making visibility
unnervingly poor when, shortly before daybreak, the corporal in
charge of the section manning the Bren gun above the rocks at the
headland sent back a runner to say they could hear what sounded

like boats' oars. They were being rowed on the seaward side of the floating boom that was winched each night across the harbour mouth. Ordering Sergeant Smith to take over and alert company HQ, I stumbled down the nearest cliff path to see for myself. The line of barrels supporting the boom was immediately below me. In the murk two unmistakable boat shapes were moving beyond it, but *towards* the sea, not away from it. Another was approaching the boom from the harbour side and I could make out figures leaning over with oars to lever the hulls over the cables.

'Who the hell are you?' My challenge being unanswered, I threatened them with a burst of fire, though I only had my revolver. Fortunately this was enough to elicit a resentful Cornish apology. They were only lobstermen going out to empty their pots. With the change in tide if they waited for the boom to be opened they'd be stranded by the low water.

BEFORE OUR WELCOME COULD TURN REALLY SOUR orders arrived for our withdrawal. The same day as I received a visit from the irate proprietor of another hotel, who also happened to be the mayor and whose daughter, he claimed, had been seduced and made pregnant by my batman, we were relieved by units from another regiment. Trucks took us to Liskeard where we joined the other companies queueing in the dusk to be issued with a twenty-four-hour ration and tropical gear, including ill-fitting khaki pith helmets. No one knew where we were being sent but by midnight we'd marched to the station for a train that took us to the docks at Liverpool.

Our chaotic embarkation in a P & O liner, partially converted into a troopship, and the voyage that followed was drawn on heavily by Waugh both in *Put Out More Flags* and *Men at Arms*. Passages of near-autobiography are embroidered and entangled with the inventions of the novelist and the demands of his plot and characters. There was nothing fictional about the military blunder that put a battalion of Highlanders into the ship meant for Cedric Lyne's unit - in fact it was the 8th Argyll and Sutherlands. It was equally true that the cargo had to be unloaded and reloaded in 'tactical order' because our main supply of ammunition lay at the bottom of the hold beneath tons of beer crates and other NAAFI comforts. True, too, were the Goanese stewards who carried on their peacetime cruising routines, calling us each morning with 'tea, an apple, a thin slice of brown bread and butter' and who announced mealtimes by walking the ship's corridors 'striking a musical gong with a little hammer'.* Like the Halberdiers we shared the ship with a 'medley of strangers - Free French liaison officers, Marine gunners, a naval beach-party, chaplains, an expert on tropical hygiene and the rest.' There was also that 'small smoking-room labelled "OPERATIONAL PLANNING. OUT OF BOUNDS TO ALL RANKS"'.† Like Crouchback I heard

Put Out More Flags, p. 182
†*Men at Arms*, p. 219

about the leaflets 'printed with the slogan:

' "FRANCAIS DE DAKAR!

' "Joignez-vous à nous pour délivrer la France.

' "GENERAL DE GAULLE." '*

Waugh might also have described how the Liverpudlian dockers pocketed souvenir de Gaulle medals spilled from a broken crate, but Dakar was only one among several rumoured destinations which included the Middle East, Ceylon, and Malaya. Hoisted on davits normally occupied by the ship's lifeboats were grey, armour-plated landing craft, but when at last we put to sea, unlike the Halberdiers we turned north instead of south and steamed through the Western Isles to spend a week at Scapa Flow.

At various points on the rim of the great inland anchorage we practised our first night assaults from landing craft. Crouched down with blackened faces we would approach a beach at speed, the rear-mounted engines suddenly going full astern as we passed through the line of breakers. The rattle of the ramp going down was the signal for me to run forward at the head of my men who fanned out on each side as they raced through the darkness for the foreshore. With luck we stepped out onto firm dry sand but sometimes the craft struck a shoal and we waded through waist-high icy water. Our last two days at Scapa were taken up with what must have been a full-scale rehearsal for the assault on Dakar. We were issued with iron rations and our equipment had been scientifically scaled down so that we could carry the maximum amount of ammunition - though I learned that Evelyn's batman struggled ashore with a knapsack containing two excellent bottles of Châteauneuf du Pape.

Eventually we rendezvoused with the other ships in the expedition and then sailed far out into the Atlantic before turning south on a zig-zagging course to mislead prowling U-boats. Among the

*Men at Arms, p. 220

convoy were ships carrying the rest of the R M brigade, the Ar-
gylls and, in two Dutch liners, some 2,500 Free French and Foreign Legion. There was also a little vessel which Waugh names
the *Belgravia* which was 'reputed to carry champagne and bath-
salts and other comforts for the garrison of Dakar'.* Two sloops,
some destroyers, and the cruiser *Fiji* formed a protective escort.

Having the run of the first-class cabins and saloons, with five-
course P & O meals and gin at a penny a tot, we officers might
have been on a hilarious luxury cruise. Even the disappearance of
the *Fiji* after being holed by a torpedo was soon forgotten in yet
another round of John Collinses. The senior NCOs were comfortable enough in the tourist class, but the other ranks were crowded
like impoverished immigrants on messdecks converted out of
cargo space. At night, rigorously battened down because of the
blackout and slung with hundreds of slowly swinging hammocks,

Men at Arms, p. 220

42

they became impossibly hot and airless. As we passed inexplicably close to the Azores (from where, no doubt, we were watched by Nazi agents), the temperature became more tropical and the men more restless. Among my own extra duties was organizing and compèring concert parties which led to my being reprimanded by the battle-eager brigadier (in the nicest possible way) for telling OR's filthy stories. I also played the only four records we had (Ivor Novello) over the ship's loudspeaker and read out the daily radioed news from which we learned of the first big London blitzes.

THE PURPOSE OF THIS SUPPOSEDLY HIGHLY SECRET
enterprise was confirmed as we anchored on September 17th off
Freetown in the mouth of the Sierra Leone river. Among the en-
circling canoes paddled by boys eager to dive for pennies and by
vendors of bananas and melons was one occupied by a laughing
African, naked apart from a dented top-hat and a placard slung
round his neck, bearing the legend:

'FUK DAKAR'

As we learned later, De Gaulle and the British war cabinet felt
that the whole of French West Africa could with luck be wrested
from Vichy's control without bloodshed. The first step was 'Operation Menace' - the occupation of Dakar. This *coup de main* would
also help deny the West African coast as a base for U-boats and
help cheer Allied morale. Another prize would be the damaged
French warship *Richelieu*. In the unlikely event of resistance the
guns of the Royal Navy and our own small landing force would be
on hand - just in case. As well as De Gaulle, the force was com-
manded by Major-General N. M. S. Irwin and Admiral J. H. D.
Cunningham, leading a fleet that contained the battleships *Barham*
and *Resolution*, three cruisers, the carrier *Ark Royal*, and a flotilla of
destroyers. While the top brass perfected their plans - and also
overcame last-minute qualms from London - our colonel decided
that a visit ashore would help to make us (literally) fighting fit.
Carrying weapons and full equipment, the whole battalion marched inland in topeed column-of-threes along roads lined with exotic
vegetation, under a brazen midday sun. As we tramped through an
occasional village the Africans gazed at us with grinning astonish-
ment from the shade of banana fronds or the entrance to a kero-
sene-tin hut. Within half-an-hour men were starting to fall out
and, despite halts, by the time we'd completed the eight-mile
circuit at least a third of the battalion were missing, to stagger back
later in the day on their own or rounded up by trucks. It took two
days, however, to re-embark the Foreign Legion: presumably they
were accustomed to the sun but, granted an afternoon's shore

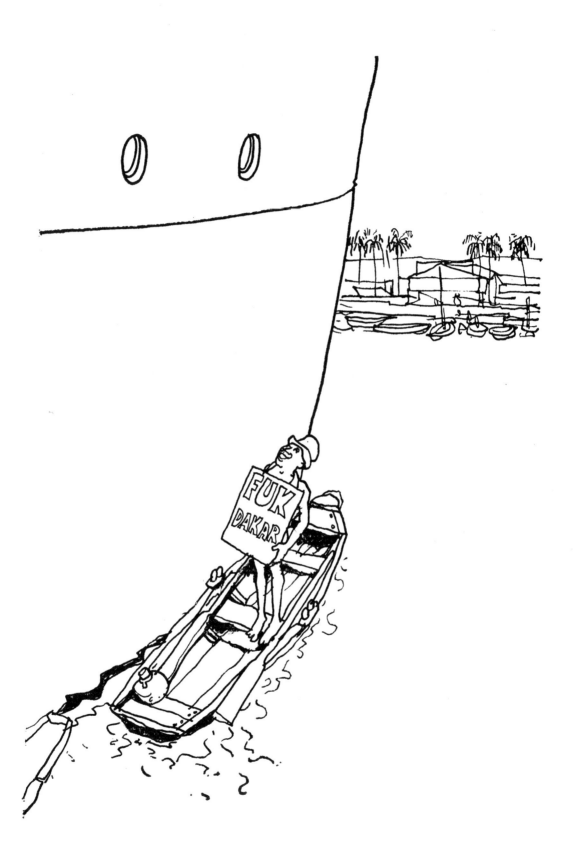

leave, they just vanished into Freetown's brothels and palm toddy shops.

Untroubled by the heat myself, I travelled the next day in the little wood-fuelled train that ran from the quayside to Freetown and accompanied Evelyn on a visit to some Irish fathers in white tropical cassocks. Afterwards we had drinks on the balcony of a sleazy fly-blown hotel that must, I'm sure, be the Bedford hotel in *The Heart of the Matter*. On the voyage out Evelyn had been depressed at having to surrender the command of his company to a regular and at being demoted to become, like Cedric Lyne, battalion Intelligence Officer, but he was soon bubbling with caustic and delighted comments on the passing life in the dilapidated, ramshackle streets; at the schoolgirls in Daniel Neal gym slips and bare feet carrying satchels on their frizzy heads; at the vultures

perched on the lych-gate of the little mock Gothic cathedral; at the
Levantine traders haggling outside their shops and the black mam-
mies in the market presiding enormously over piles of yams and
cheap crockery. The younger Freetown women were resplendent
in wraps of vividly patterned cotton. Balancing head bundles, they
strolled often with a sleeping child strapped to backs erect above
incredibly swaying hips, their skins ranging from purplish black
through every shade of sienna to the gentlest ochre. They were all
that I'd imagined and so were the palms and bougainvillaea, the
men's ivory smiles, the noisy talk and laughter, and yet . . . and yet
there were all those neglected deformities, the soap-eyed stares of
the blind, the place's sheer poverty. This became clearer the next
day when I took my platoon to bathe from a beach near the outskirts. From the jungly foreshore emerged a middle-aged African
lady, dressed respectably as if for chapel and followed by two gig-
gly teenage daughters. Having made sure that I was the officer-in-
charge, she offered their services at fourpence a turn.

AFTER A FEW DAYS WE AWOKE TO FIND OURSELVES at sea again, steaming north. This was it. But by the time we were twenty miles off Dakar visibility was reduced to a few yards by fog - as thick as in London but white and stagnant: as Crouchback noted, 'there was an odd smell, identified as that of groundnuts, borne to them from the near but invisible coast.'* The fog was unexpected and, as it turned out, disastrous. It typified all that happened during the next anxious three days. Another disaster was the then inexplicable blunder by the garrison at Gibraltar of permitting three Vichy cruisers and three destroyers from Toulon to slip unmolested out of the Mediterranean; below decks they were stuffed with embittered Vichy partisans and shells for the Dakar shore batteries and the 15-inch guns of the *Richelieu*; their arrival had done much to overawe the wavering French colonials.

Our ship churned an endless circle through the fog. Farewell letters to wives and sweethearts were handed to the chaplain and we awaited the orders to man the landing craft. De Gaulle and the French troops were meanwhile waiting to be put ashore some twenty miles farther south - out of wireless reach, we learned later, of the British admiral's flagship. Rumours, some of which turned out to be true, trickled from the out-of-bounds smoking-room. The operation had been started by planes scattering leaflets printed in the colours of the Tricolor and by De Gaulle radioing a proclamation to the governor-general and inhabitants. He had come to deliver them with the support of a considerable Allied force, amounting to no less than thirty-five vessels but, alas, it appeared that no one was very impressed, maybe because the fog hid us so completely. A Free French delegation then landed at Dakar's airport, only to be arrested with lists of Gaullist sympathisers in their pockets. A second delegation in motorboats flying white flags was rejected after a short parley and, as it left, was machine-gunned, two members being seriously wounded. We heard later that a pro-Gaullist demonstration by Africans as well as Europeans had been

Men at Arms, p. 221

50

suppressed brutally. The Free French were therefore no doubt justified in next attempting their beach landing at Rufisque farther down the coast but, denied by the fog support from the fleet's guns and Swordfish aircraft, and fired upon from the land, they hastily re-embarked.

The second day began with an ultimatum after which the British ships opened a bombardment of the city and port, their aim hampered by the fog. A native hospital was damaged and there were considerable civilian casualties. The Vichy warships were also said to have been hit, though they weren't slow to return our fire. Waugh reports a 'rumour that *Barham* was holed. A little Unfree French aeroplane droned out of the clouds and dropped a bomb very near them.'* The Vichy governor-general radioed back indignantly that La France 'has placed Dakar in my care. I shall defend her to the end. I leave you the responsibility for the bloodshed.'

As we listened to the cannonade, our ship still circling in the fog, a sick dry fear crawled along my limbs at the knowledge of my coming personal involvement in action, the moment for which throughout the 'thirties each newspaper report, each slogan chalked on the sooty London walls – 'Fascism means war!' – each quarrel with my parents over Munich and Chamberlain had been preparing me . . . and yet I now understood what people meant when they spoke of events seeming as if they were happening to someone else. In a waking dream I repeated once more the memorised battle plans and the maps of the beach-head allocated to my platoon; our first objective was a road on the far side of a public garden – this might mean crossing an ornamental lake and so we had to bring ashore an inflatable dinghy; there would certainly also be barbed wire which we planned to cut through with Bangalore torpedoes, eight-foot metal pipes packed with gelignite . . . but the Goanese stewards still walked the corridors with their little gongs to announce the five-course *table d'hôte*. Ivor Novello's

Men at Arms, p. 222

Dancing Years still poured their reassuring syrup through the ship's loudspeakers.

On the third morning, September 25th, the British bombardment reopened in clearer weather. If it failed to force a surrender, we would make our assault. During the night a message from Churchill in Downing Street had urged the expedition to complete its mission, to 'stop at nothing'. All morning we waited in the stagnant heat. Once we paraded by the sally port, fully equipped and ready to clamber into the landing craft, but then there was another postponement. The ship churned round the same circle. Few of us could face another lunch. Then, suddenly, unbelievably it was off! We were steaming full speed ahead in a straight line south and out to sea. The *Cumberland* had been severely damaged and the *Resolution* torpedoed - as the mists lifted, we could see her being taken in tow, heeled over to port, her great guns pointing to starboard to stop her turning turtle. A landing now would certainly be opposed and Dakar occupied only at the cost of heavy casualties. The commanders on the spot had reached their own decision. We were running away.

The gins in the officers' saloon that evening were swallowed more quickly than ever with a heavy show of frustration and disappointment. Secretly I was light-headed with relief, though until then I hadn't been aware of the extent of my fright. Shit scared. I doubt if I was the only one. When Crouchback was told to break the news of the withdrawal to his men ' ". . . and keep their spirit up." There was little need for this order. Surprisingly a spirit of boisterous fun possessed the ship.'*

*Men at Arms, p. 222

53

Though no more than a skirmish, worth only a few pages in the war histories, Dakar was the nearest I ever came to the enemy. Despite joining such a hazardous-sounding unit I never fired a shot in action. Like many thousands of British troops, my lot somehow missed all the 'big parties'. Back in Scotland, by way of Gibraltar, we planned and rehearsed the occupation of the Azores, of Madeira, and elsewhere; we embarked on other troopships, their davits festooned with landing craft, but always at the last minute we were called back. Much of our time was spent at Inverary at the head of Loch Fyne, then the Combined Operations Training Centre. Inverary undoubtedly inspired much of what occurred on the Isle of Mugg, though Evelyn by then had transferred to another battalion. Those deer shot by tommy guns belonged, we were told, to the Duke of Argyll; they just happened to canter in front of our sights during a rain-soaked morning on the field firing range.

Eventually our battalion split up and before the war ended quite a few of us, both regular and temporary, were to be wounded or die on beaches swept by fire and terror that even Cinerama or Panavision could never recreate. Our adjutant was taken prisoner during the landing at Dieppe. Evelyn took part in the evacuation from Crete: his description of the cowardice of the discomforted regular, Major Fido Hound, was matched by his own bravery under fire which was said to have been remarkable. But for many of us only a very small part of our years in uniform, or no part at all, was spent attacking or defending ourselves in the face of a live enemy. Like the civilians, we followed the course of the war on the radio and in the censored press and we attended current affairs talks in Nissen huts, but we were seldom, if at all, conscious of being the gallant defenders of civilisation. Our preoccupations were more personal: the date of our next spell of duty as orderly officer; a worrying letter from home; a five bob win on last night's housey-housey; the breasts of the soubrette in the monthly ENSA concert party . . . and of course the size of the next issue of fags and the number of weeks before our next forty-eight hour leave on the spree in the London blitz.

54

At any rate this was what military service meant to me, especially during the early months. Evelyn got their mood just right. The officers' mess of the Halberdiers may offer too narrow, too privileged a viewpoint and the magnitude of Europe's agony only occasionally pervades his pages, yet his observation is meticulous and completely honest. Evelyn describes the war as I experienced it. Nothing is falsified. One may have little sympathy for his celebrated patrician social posture or for his ultra High Tory political prejudices, and yet in his treatment of Guy Crouchback he had the courage to expose, to ridicule many of what must have been his own illusions. Though for Evelyn the old-style aristocratic, romantic devotion to God and Honour remained a valid ideal, it is not only his middle- and lower-class characters who act out their own condemnation. Emerging from the whole *Sword of Honour* trilogy is the futility of much of the war effort, the disenchantment with killing, the inevitable betrayal of civilized values. Some of these collapsing values reflected merely his idiosyncratic, ritualist obscurantism, and yet how right he was to avoid treating 1939-45 as an epic; instead he unmasked it as an ironic series of muddled, sordid, often cruel and pointless episodes that released men's most unattractive and ridiculous qualities. In *Unconditional Surrender*, the last volume in the trilogy, Evelyn's dislike of the partisans and the 'People's War' may at times betray a pathological pessimism and even be unpleasantly old-maidish, but he expresses the disillusions of many of us when he gets a displaced Jewish refugee to say to Guy: ' "... It seems to me there was a will to war, a death wish, everywhere. Even good men thought their private honour would be satisfied by war. They could assert their manhood by killing and being killed. They would accept hardships in recompense for having been selfish and lazy. Danger justified privilege. I knew Italians - not very many perhaps - who felt like this. Were there none in England?"

' "God forgive me," said Guy. "I was one of them." '*

Waugh's novels are a splendid antidote to the glamorised, lying versions of the war that are now the mode. They provide the truest as well as the funniest guide to what it was really like.

*Unconditional Surrender, p. 232

This edition of 600 copies was printed by L E S L I E
J O H N   R A N D L E, R O S A L I N D   R A N D L E *and*
C H A R L E S   L O W N D E S *at Whittington Court,
Gloucestershire. The type is hand-set in* 12-*pt Caslon,
and the paper is T. H. Saunders' Mould Made Blue
Laid from Wookey Hole Mill, Somerset. The line
blocks were made by Craske, Vaus & Crampton Ltd,
and the William Morris Willow Bough material
used on the binding of the cloth copies was supplied by
Arthur Sanderson & Sons Ltd. The endpapers were
marbled by Charles Lowndes, and the books were
bound by Hunter & Foulis Ltd, Edinburgh.*

Printing completed February 1973.

This is copy no. 507